THE NEW **anchor** BOOK OF
Free-Style Embroid

D1150169

& Charles

Compiled by Eve Harlow

Contents

Introduction

This new book of free-style embroidery stitches will be useful to anyone who is interested in embroidery — not just teachers and students, but to needlewomen everywhere.

It will also be of particular interest to beginners, who may want to increase their 'repertoire' of stitches.

The stitches are set out in alphabetical order so that you can quickly locate a particular stitch. The colour photographs show the finished effect of the stitch and how it can be combined with other stitches to create attractive motifs.

Any of the motifs in this book can be used to decorate clothes, accessories or home furnishings and, at the back of the book, life-size trace-off patterns are provided for you.

1

Antwerp Edging

Also known as Knot Stitch Edging, this is one of the many forms of Knot Stitches used in embroidery. It is mostly used to give a decorative edge to a finished hem.

Flower Edging

The design opposite is worked in Back Stitch, Satin Stitch, Double Knot Stitch and Chain Stitch and finished with Antwerp Edging, worked in Pearl Cotton 01. Stranded Embroidery Cotton is used to work the solid areas.

This design could be used for the corner of a tray cloth or for a tablecloth. A continuous edging motif could be obtained by reversing the fuchsia flower so that the stem ends touch and perhaps setting the four-petalled flower between pairs of fuchsias.

Fig 1 Hold down the thread end with a thumb and insert the needle at A, bringing the needle through to the back of the fabric and keeping the working thread under the needle point.

Fig 2 Still holding the thread end down, pull the working thread to form a twisted loop, then pass the needle behind the twisted loop, keeping the working thread under the needle point.

Fig 3 Pull the thread firmly to set the knot and insert the needle at B. Continue as shown in Fig 2.

Fig 4 The finished effect of Antwerp Edging. To finish off the thread ends, darn them between the layers of the hem.

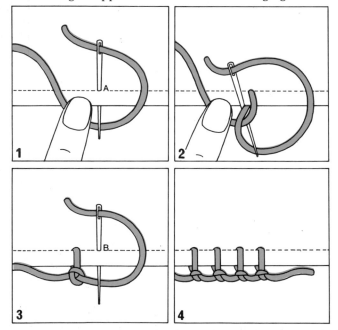

Flower Edging ▶
A trace-off pattern for this design is on page 98

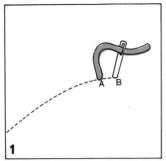

Back Stitch

Back Stitch is one of the straight stitches and is most often used as an outlining stitch, although it can also form the basis for other decorative stitches. It is one of the main stitches used in Black Work, worked on evenweave fabric.

Ring of Birds

This charming design uses only three stitches, Satin Stitch, French Knots and Back Stitch. Stranded Cotton was used, colours 0303, 0890, 0104, 0110, 0433, 0410 and 0403.

Five birds in a circle make a central motif for a cushion or a tablecloth. A single bird could be worked on a scarf or pocket.

Fig 1 Bring the needle through at A and insert the needle at B.

Fig 2 Bring the needle out at C (the distance between C-A and A-B should be equal).

Fig 3 Re-insert the needle at A, making sure the needle is inserted exactly in the hole previously made.

Fig 4 Bring the needle out at D, keeping the distance between D-C the same as the length of previous stitches.

Fig 5 Re-insert the needle at C, in exactly the same hole as previously made.

Ring of Birds ▶

A trace-off pattern for this bird is on page 100

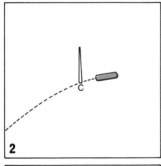

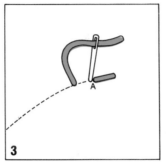

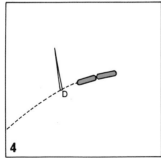

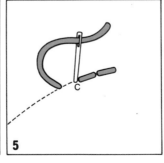

4

Bokhara Couching

Bokhara Couching is one of several types of couching but differs in that only one length of thread is used for both the laying and the couching.

Happy Bear
In this design, Bokhara Couching is used on the bear's trousers, using Tapisserie Wool, colour 0145.

Fig 1 Bring the thread though at A, insert the needle at B. Bring the needle out at C.

Fig 2 Insert the needle at D and bring it out at E, forming a small, sloping, tying stitch.

Fig 3 Insert the needle at F and bring it out at G.

Fig 4 Insert the needle at H and bring it out at I.

Fig 5 Insert the needle at J and bring it out at K.

Fig 6 The finished effect, where the laid threads are tied down at even intervals.

Happy Bear ▶
A trace-off pattern for the bear is on page 99

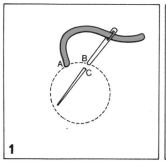

1

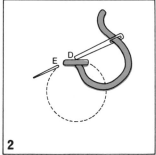

2

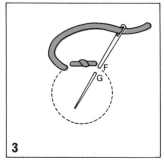

3

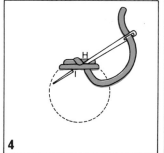

4

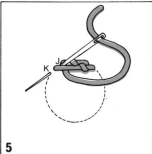

5

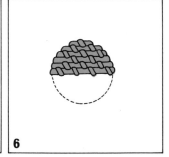

6

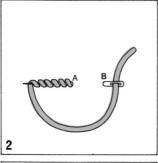

1

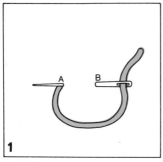

2

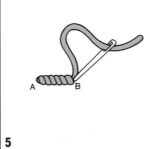

3

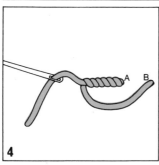

4

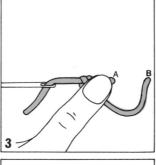

5

Bullion Stitch

This is one of the detached stitches with a raised effect. It can be used in a massed effect, as shown in the hair of the girl pictured, or singly.

Girl with Balloons

This design uses several stitches, each of them chosen to produce the desired texture – Satin Stitch, Stem Stitch, Buttonhole Stitch, a French Knot and Bullion Stitch.

Fig 1 *Bring the thread through at A, insert the needle at B and bring out again at A, taking a back stitch the size of Bullion Stitch required. Do not pull the needle right through the fabric.*

Fig 2 *Twist the thread around the needle point five or six times, depending on the length of the stitch from A-B.*

Fig 3 *Hold a thumb on the coiled thread and pull the needle through, taking care not to distort the twists.*

Fig 4 *The needle pulled through.*

Fig 5 *Insert the needle again at B and pull the working thread until the Bullion Stitch lies flat.*

Girl with Balloons ▶
A trace-off pattern for this design is on page 102

8

Buttonhole Stitch

This is one of the large group of loop stitches and can be worked in straight lines, along curves or in rings or wheels. It is sometimes used, with Running Stitch, in cutwork or open-work embroidery.

Cutwork Corner

Cutwork can look lacy and delicate but it will stand up to wear and to laundering, making it ideal for decorating table and bed linens, as well as clothing. The floral corner pictured is worked in Pearl Cotton No 8, colour 0387 for the Buttonhole Stitch and Stranded Cotton, colour 0367 for the other stitches.

Fig 1 *Bring the needle through on the bottom design line at A. Insert the needle at B on the top design line and slightly to the right, and bring it out at C, directly below. Before pulling the needle through, take the thread under the needle point.*

Fig 2 *Pull the thread through to form the stitch. Insert the needle at D on the top design line and bring it out at E, immediately below, with the thread under the needle point.*

Fig 3 *Continue working stitches as shown F-G, keeping the depth of the stitches even.*

Fig 4 *Place stitches very close together to make a firm edge. In cutwork, the loops are set on the edge to be cut.*

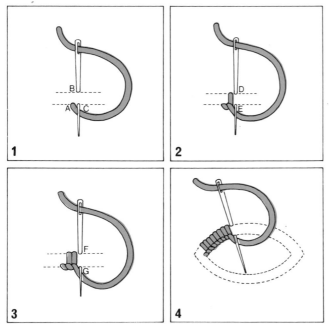

Cutwork corner ▶
A trace-off pattern for this design is on page 100

Buttonhole Stitch Bar

Bars are used for pattern linking in cutwork such as the antennae in the butterfly opposite.

Cutwork Butterfly

The motif pictured is worked in Buttonhole Stitch using white Pearl Cotton No. 8. Stranded Cotton is used for the Satin Stitch, Stem Stitch and Buttonhole Bars.

Fig 1 Bring the needle through at A, insert the needle at B, take a small downward stitch and bring it out at C.

Fig 2 Insert the needle again at A and bring it out at D.

Figs 3, 4 and 5 *Follow the instructions for Buttonhole Stitch (page 10, Figs 1, 2 and 3), working the stitches over the threads without piercing the fabric.*

Fig 6 *The completed bar.*

Cutwork Butterfly ▶

A trace-off pattern for this design is on page 101

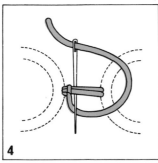

1

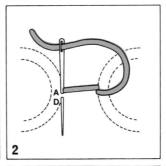

2

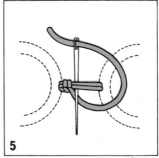

3

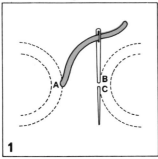

4

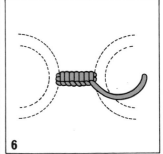

5

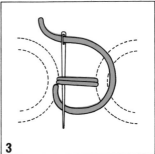

6

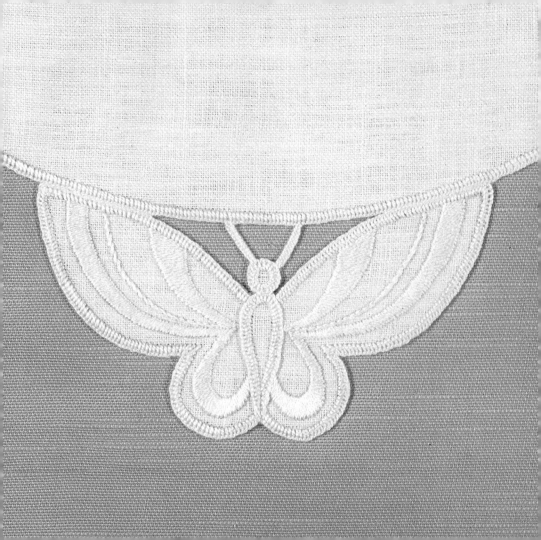

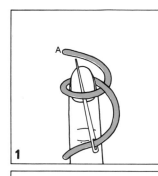

1

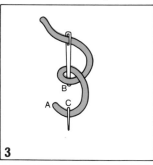

2

3

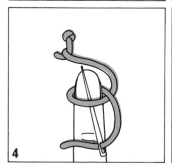

4

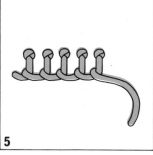

5

Knotted Buttonhole Stitch

This is another of the stitches in the Blanket Stitch group and has a knot at the top of each stitch.

Corner Scroll
This decorative motif is designed to be worked on the corner of a piece of fabric, or it could be used for a border design.

Chain Stitch, Satin Stitch, Jacobean Couching and Knotted Buttonhole Stitch are used.

Fig 1 Bring the thread through at A and make a loop from right to left over the thumb. Then insert the needle point upwards, under the loop, as shown.

Fig 2 Slip the loop on to the needle and, with the loop still around the needle, insert the needle at B.

Fig 3 Bring the needle out at C, keeping the thread under the point and, before pulling the needle through the fabric, tighten the loop around the head of the needle by pulling the working thread.

Fig 4 Pull the needle through to form the stitch, then make a loop over the thumb in readiness for the next stitch.

Fig 5 A finished row of Knotted Buttonhole Stitches.

Corner Scroll ▶
A trace-off pattern for this design is on page 101

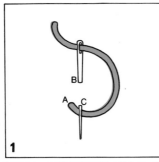

1

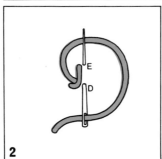

2

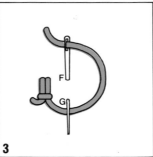

3

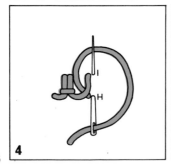

4

5

Up and Down Buttonhole Stitch

Another variation of Buttonhole Stitch that makes a pretty edging but can also be used to lighten the edges of a design when used as in the Jacobean Motif opposite for the flower and leaf forms on the left.

This traditional, stylised motif uses five different stitches: Chain Stitch, Stem Stitch, Fly Stitch, French Knots, Back Stitch and Up and Down Buttonhole Stitch. A closely-matched range of Stranded Cottons is used, colours 09, 0338, 0340, 042 and 043.

Fig 1 *Bring the thread through at A. Insert the needle at B and bring it out at C, immediately below, keeping the thread under the needle point.*

Fig 2 *Insert the needle at D and bring it out at E, with the thread under the needle point. Pull the thread through first in an upward movement, then downwards in readiness for the next stitch.*

Fig 3 *Insert the needle at F and bring it out at G.*

Fig 4 *Insert the needle at H and bring it out at I.*

Fig 5 *Insert the needle at J and bring it out at K. Continue, working in sequence, spacing stitches evenly.*

Jacobean Motif ▶

A trace-off pattern for this design is on page 105

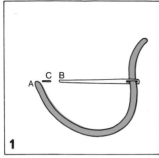

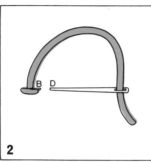

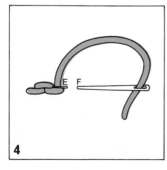

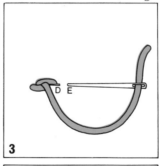

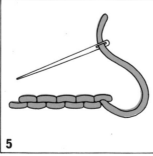

Cable Stitch

Cable Stitch can be used as an edging stitch (it outlines the house pictured), as a filling stitch, massed in rows, and it is also one of the firm control stitches used in smocking.

Little House

The little house design makes an ideal picture for framing for a child's room. Enlarged photographically, the motif has an even wider application, for cushions or for other home accessories. Other forms of decorative stitchery could be used also, the design lending itself to interpretation into appliqué or even quilting.

Fig 1 *Bring the needle through at A. Keeping the thread below the needle, insert the needle at B and bring it out at C, midway between A and B.*

Fig 2 *From C, work the next stitch in the same way, but keep the thread above the needle, inserting the needle at D and bringing it out at B.*

Fig 3 *Insert the needle at E and bring it out at D.*

Fig 4 *Insert the needle at F and bring it out at E.*

Fig 5 *The finished effect of Cable Stitch.*

Little House ▶

A trace-off pattern for this design is on page 104

18

Cable Chain Stitch

This is one of the variations of Chain Stitch and has the look of a linked chain. It has been used as an outlining stitch in the Aeroplanes design opposite, (used to outline the clouds), but it also looks effective worked in close or spaced massed bands.

Aeroplanes

This design of two monoplanes flying in clouds could be worked as a picture for a boy's room or as a motif for a T-shirt or for nightwear. The design is also simple enough to be enlarged and used for appliqué.

Fig 1 Bring the thread through at A and hold it down with the thumb. Without piercing the fabric, pass the needle from right to left under the working thread.

Fig 2 Twist the needle back to the right over the working thread, and still holding the thread with the thumb, insert the needle at B, bringing it out at C. Keeping the thread under the needle point, pull the working thread to form a chain loop.

Fig 3 Following Figs 1 and 2 for procedure, insert the needle at D and bring it out at E.

Fig 4 The finished effect when the loops are firmly pulled to form a chain.

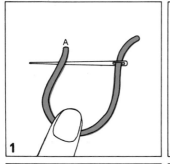

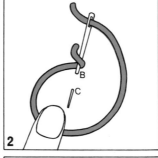

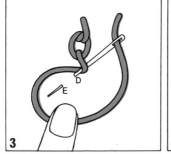

Aeroplanes ▶
A trace-off pattern for this design is on page 103

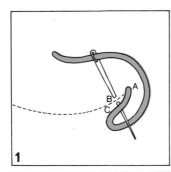

1

Knotted Cable Chain Stitch

This is a variation on Cable Chain Stitch, with a decorative knot worked in each chain link. In the stylised flower design opposite, the stitch has been used to outline the petals and for the stems.

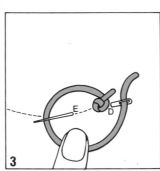

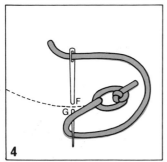

2

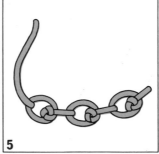

3

4

5

Art Nouveau

This is typical of the stylised flower and leaf forms which can be used on home furnishings.

Fig 1 Bring the thread through at A on the design line and insert it at B, bringing it out at C. Wrap the thread over and under the needle point as shown.

Fig 2 Pull the thread through to form a knot, then slip the needle under the stitch between the knot and A, without piercing the fabric.

Fig 3 Pull the thread through, insert the needle at D and bring it out at E, with the thread under the needle point, and hold it down with the thumb. Pull through to form a chain.

Fig 4 Insert the needle at F and bring it out at G, then wrap the thread over and under the needle to start the next stitch.

Fig 5 The finished effect of Knotted Cable Chain Stitches.

Art Nouveau ▶
A trace-off pattern for this design is on page 107

A trace-off pattern for this design is on page 107

22

Chain Stitch

Chain stitch can be used as an outline stitch or worked in close rows as a filling.

Fig 1 Bring the thread through at A, hold the thread down with the thumb and insert the needle through the same hole at A.

Fig 2 Bring the needle out at B and, keeping the thread under the needle point, pull the loop of thread to form a chain.

Fig 3 Hold the thread down with the thumb and insert the needle down through the same hole at B.

Fig 4 As Fig 2, bringing the needle out at C.

Fig 5 Hold the thread down with the thumb and insert the needle down through the same hole at C. Continue working stitches in the same way.

Fig 6 Finishing the last loop with a small tying stitch.

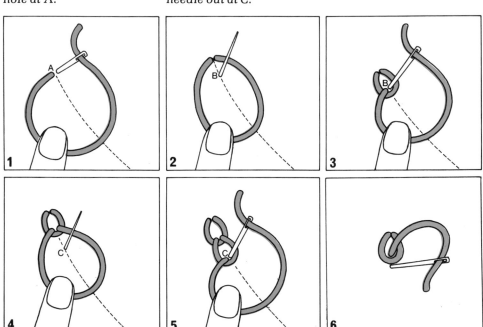

Chain Stitch, Open

Open Chain Stitch is one of the many variations of Chain Stitch and is also known as Square Chain or Ladder Chain Stitch.

In the Pear design, Open Chain Stitch is used to define design lines but it can also be worked as a filling stitch in rows, or can be worked to varying widths to fill a shape.

Pear and Apples

The Pear, and the Apples design on page 25, would make an attractive set of matched pictures, or they could each be used as a motif for table mats or for a trolley cloth.

Enlarged to about 25cm (10in) deep, the designs would also look effective worked for cushions, perhaps using Tapisserie Wool.

The Pear is worked in three stitches: Satin Stitch for the solid areas, with Back and Open Chain Stitches defining design lines.

Fig 1 *Bring the thread through at A and insert the needle a short distance to the right at B, and bring it out at C, holding the thread down with the thumb and under the needle point, leaving the loop slightly loose.*

Fig 2 *Insert the needle at D and bring out at E.*

Fig 3 *Insert the needle at F and bring out at G.*

Fig 4 *Shows the finished effect. Secure the last stitch with a small loop at each side.*

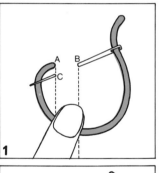

1

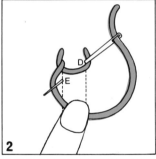

2

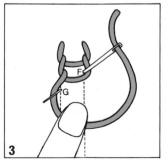

3

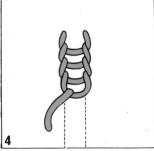

4

Pear ▶
A trace-off pattern for this design is on page 107

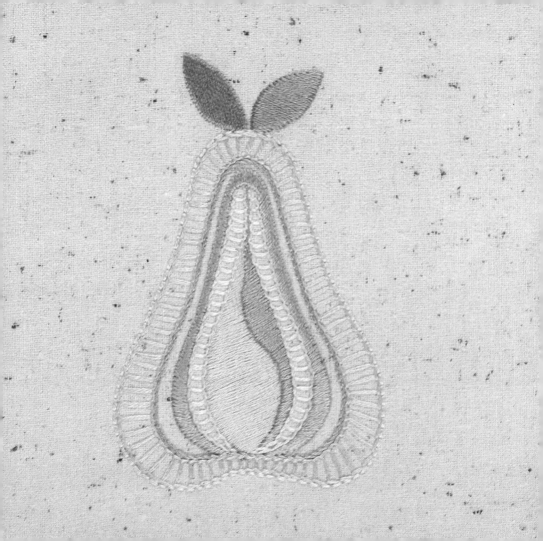

Rosette Chain Stitch

This pretty variation of Chain Stitch can be used to outline a design, as shown in the corner motif opposite, or it can be worked in straight rows or, even, in circles. The motif pictured is worked in Soft Embroidery thread but it could also be worked in Tapisserie Wool for a chunkier effect, such as might be required on a denim skirt or on a jacket.

Worked in Stranded Cotton or Pearl Cotton, the stitch would have a delicate effect on fine fabrics.

Fig 1 Bring the thread through at A and insert the needle at B. Bring the needle out at C, then wrap the thread over and under the needle point as shown.

Fig 2 Pull the thread through to form a twisted loop, then slip the needle under the thread between the twist and A, without piercing the fabric.

Fig 3 Pull the thread through, taking care not to pull the thread too tightly, then insert the needle at D and bring it out at E. Continue working in sequence.

Fig 4 The finished effect when worked straight as a border.

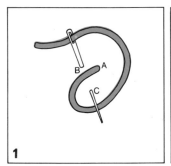

1

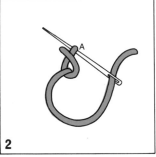

2

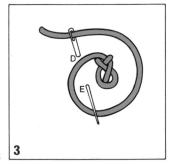

3

4

Corner motif ▶
A trace-off pattern for this design is on page 109

28

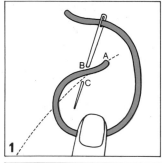

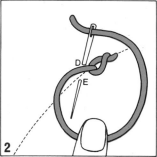

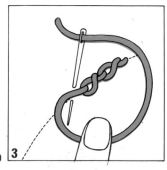

Chain Stitch, Twisted

Another variation of Chain Stitch, Twisted Chain Stitch is a decorative outlining stitch, providing textural interest when used in simple outlined designs.

Worked in close rows, the stitch can simulate a braid edging along the edge of a garment, particularly when worked in wool.

Another interesting braid effect is achieved when Twisted Chain Stitch is worked over two close rows of Buttonhole Stitch.

Shells

The design is worked in a range of pastel colours in Stranded Cotton, 0161, 02, 0885, 4146, 0778, 0890 and 0886 and 0831, using Stem Stitch, Back Stitch, Twisted Chain Stitch, and French Knots.

As there are no solid areas in the design, Shells could be worked on quite coarse fabrics, such as denim or heavy cotton, decorating a beach bag or a jacket and skirt. The design would also be suitable for a set of patio cushions, perhaps enlarged to about 20cm (8in) wide. This type of linear design is ideal for working on huckaback linen towels and a single colour or two toning colours might be used for a co-ordinated scheme.

Fig 1 *Bring the thread through at A, hold it down with the thumb, insert the needle a little to the left at B, take a small, slanting stitch across the line of the design (keeping the thread under the needle point) and bring the needle out at C.*

Fig 2 *Pull the thread up to form a twisted chain, hold it down with the thumb, insert the needle at D and bring it out at E.*

Fig 3 *Pull the thread through to form a twisted chain, and then continue, following the sequence. The stitches should be worked close together to create the right effect.*

Shells ▶

A trace-off pattern for this design is on page 109

Chained Feather Stitch

This stitch is one of the Feather Stitch family, with a chained variation. The border on the opposite page is worked with a selection of stitches from earlier pages.

Fig 1 Bring the thread through at A and make a slanting Chain Stitch (see pages 24–25); bring the thread through at B. Take the small slanting stitch C-D (D is level with B).

Fig 2 Holding the thread down with the thumb, re-insert the needle at D and bring it out again at C.

Fig 3 Keeping the thread under the needle point, pull the thread through at C and insert the needle at E (immediately down from B) and bring it out at F (on the same level as C and immediately below A).

Figs 4 and 5 Work as for Figs 1, 2 and 3, following the sequence and forming a zigzag pattern.

Fig 6 The finished effect.

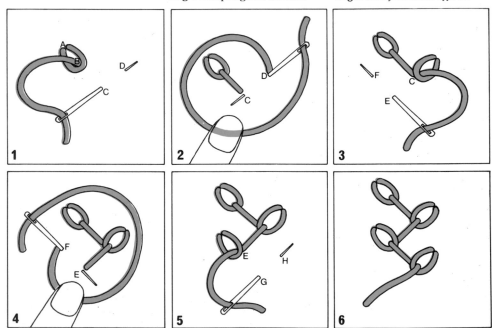

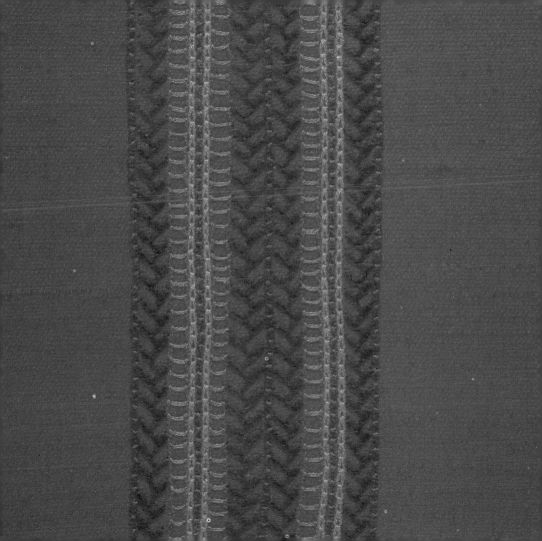

Chevron Stitch

This stitch is worked between two design lines, and is used both as a border or as a filling stitch (see Emily's bonnet opposite).

Fig 1 Bring the thread through at A on the lower design line, insert the needle at B and take a small stitch, bringing the needle out at C (half way between A and B). Keep the thread below the needle.

Fig 2 Insert the needle at D on the upper design line, take a small stitch and bring it out at E.

Fig 3 Insert the needle at F, with the thread above the needle, and bring it out again at D.

Fig 4 Insert the needle at G on the lower design line, and bring it out again at H.

Fig 5 Insert the needle at I and bring it out at G.

Fig 6 On the upper design line, insert the needle at J and bring it out at K.

Emily with flowers ▶
A trace-off pattern for this design is on page 99

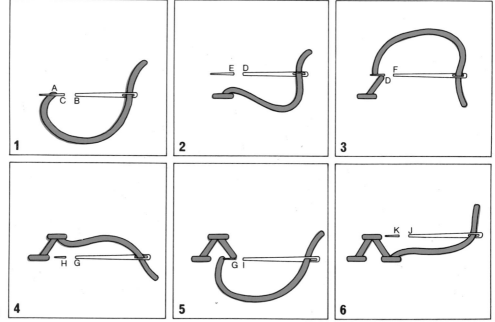

Couching

Couching or couched work is a technique in which a thread is laid along the design line and is held in place with stitches worked with a second thread. The second thread is sometimes in a contrasting colour – or texture – and the decorative effect can be seen in the leaf design opposite where threads have been couched down with threads of a lighter colour.

Leaf Motif

The Leaf is worked in a range of autumn colours in Stranded Cotton, from a yellow, colour 0311, to the warmer tones of 0314, 0324 and 0339, together with Soft Embroidery Thread in colour 0341.

Satin Stitch is used for the solid areas, with Stem Stitch and Back Stitch contrasting in texture with the couched threads.

Fig 1 *Bring the thread through at A and lay it along the line of the design.*

Fig 2 *Hold the laid thread in position with the thumb and with another thread in the needle, bring the thread through at B and insert it at C, to form a small Straight Stitch, or tying stitch, across the laid thread.*

Fig 3 *Bring the thread through at D and insert the needle at E. Continue working in this way.*

Fig 4 *Shows the finished effect with the laid thread tied down at regular intervals.*

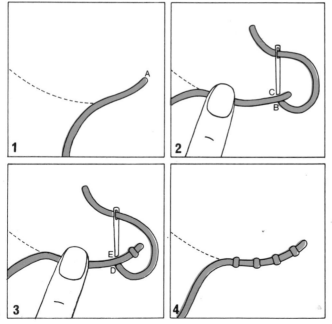

Leaf Motif ▶
A trace-off pattern for this design is on page 108

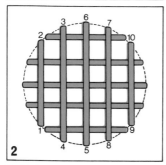

Couching, Jacobean

Jacobean Couching is a filling stitch, and is used to fill a variety of shapes in Jacobean embroidery. Here, it is used to depict the basket texture in the Basket of Flowers motif on the opposite page.

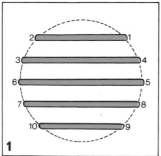

1

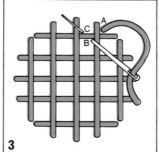

2

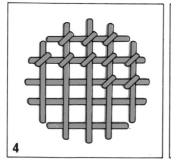

3

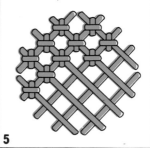

4

5

Fig 1 To prepare for couching, work long, evenly spaced Straight Stitches, (laid threads), across the shape horizontally as shown, following the numerical sequence.

Fig 2 Work long, evenly spaced Straight Stitches down the shape, vertically, following the numerical sequence.

Fig 3 The laid threads are tied down at all intersections with small, diagonal stitches. Bring the thread through at A, insert the needle at B, diagonally over the intersection of laid threads, and bring it out at C in readiness for the next stitch.

Fig 4 Continue working these half Cross Stitches, from right to left, then left to right on the next row as shown.

Fig 5 Laid threads can also be set diagonally on a shape and the intersections tied down with a small Cross Stitch.

Basket of Flowers ▶
A trace-off pattern for this design is on page 102

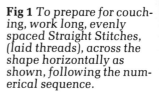

38

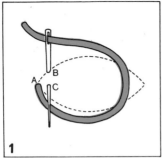

Cretan Stitch

This is one of the family of Feather Stitches and is often used as a filling for leaf shapes. A plait effect is formed down the middle of the stitch.

Leaf Border

This elegant-looking border is ideally suited to table linens or guest towels, but could be used for any furnishings or accessories where a decorative border effect is required.

The embroidery pictured is worked in Stranded Cotton in a soft, subtle colour scheme, 0311, 0891 and 0890 for the leaves and stems, with Pearl Cotton in colour 0168 for the edging.

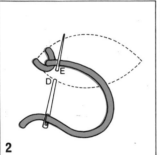

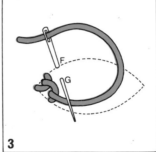

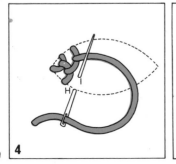

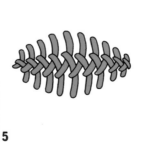

Fig 1 *Bring the thread through at A and insert the needle at B, bringing it out at C with the thread under the needle point.*

Fig 2 *Pull the thread up to form a loop and insert the needle at D and bring it out at E, with the thread under the needle point.*

Fig 3 *The next stage, F-G, is worked as Fig 1, following the curve of the design.*

Fig 4 *Continue in sequence, with H-I worked as Fig 2.*

Fig 5 *The finished effect of the stitch worked in a leaf shape.*

Leaf Border ▶
A trace-off pattern for this design is on page 110

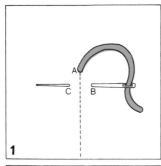

1

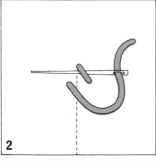

2

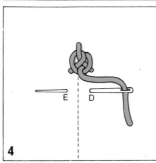

3

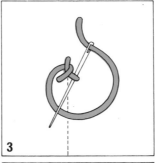

4

5

Double Knot Stitch

One of the many Knot Stitches, Double Knot Stitch is also known as Double Coral Knot, Palestrina Knot, Smyrna Knot and Old English Knot.

Scroll Motif
The formal design pictured on the opposite page would be suitable for using as a single motif on table linens or bed linens. Both Tapisserie Wool and Stranded Cotton have been used in the embroidery, with Satin Stitch for the solid areas.

Fig 1 *Bring the thread through at A on the design line and insert the needle at B, bringing it out at C to form a small Straight Stitch.*

Fig 2 *Pass the needle behind the Straight Stitch without piercing the fabric.*

Fig 3 *Pull the thread through and pass the needle behind the lower half of the stitch, without piercing the fabric and keeping the thread under the needle point. Pull the thread through to form a knot.*

Fig 4 *Insert the needle at D and bring it out at E in readiness for the next stitch.*

Fig 5 *The finished effect of a row of Double Knot Stitches.*

Scroll Motif ▶
A trace-off pattern for this design is on page 110

Feather Stitch

Feather Stitch has a wide range of applications in embroidery. It was one of the stitches used to decorate work smocks in the eighteenth and nineteenth centuries, together with Chain Stitch and Buttonhole Stitch, and is still used to decorate hems and edges on children's clothes and babies' clothes. Feather Stitch is sometimes used in quilting and appliqué decoration.

Feather Stitch Panel

The decorative border opposite shows the effect of massed rows of Feather Stitch and other stitches. Work the panel on a dress yoke or as a band on the hem of a peasant-type skirt. It would also look effective on placemats or on cushions.

From the outside edge to the middle as follows: Cable Chain Stitch (2 rows), Feather Stitch, Chain Stitch, Open Chain Stitch, Cable Chain Stitch (2 rows), Feather Stitch, Chain Stitch, Open Chain Stitch. The order is then reversed, omitting the centre row.

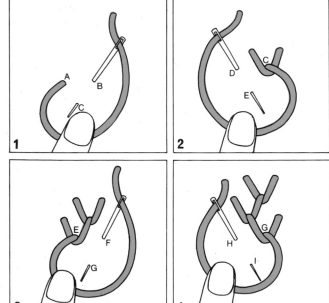

Fig 1 *Stitches are worked from top to bottom. Bring thread through at A and insert the needle at B on the same level, bringing it out at C. The distance between A-B-C should be the same.*

Fig 2 *Keeping the thread below the needle, insert the needle at D and bring it out at E. The distance between C-D-E should be the same.*

Fig 3 *Work stitch F-G, as Fig 1, keeping the thread below the needle.*

Fig 4 *Work stitch H-I as Fig 2. To end a row of stitches, take the thread over the last loop.*

Feather Stitch Panel ▶

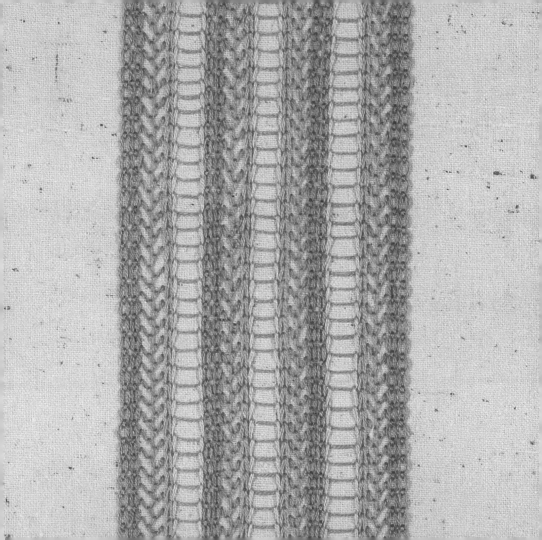

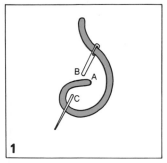

4

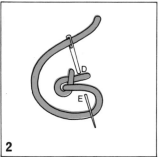

3

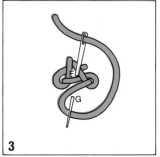

2

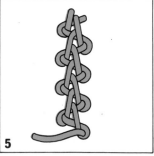

1

5

Feather Stitch, Spanish Knotted

This stitch is one of the varieties of Feather Stitch and produces a complex but very effective line of stitches.

Tulip Head

This flower design uses the decorative effect of Spanish Knotted Feather Stitch to define the flower's petals, with Satin Stitch, Back Stitch, Chain Stitch and French Knots for contrast.

Fig 1 Bring the needle through at A, insert the needle at B and bring it through at C. B is above and slightly to the left of A, C is diagonally lower and to the left of A. Wrap the thread over and under the needle point as shown.

Fig 2 Pull the thread through and insert the needle at D and bring it out at E. Wrap the thread over and under the needle point.

Fig 3 Pull the thread through and insert the needle at F, bringing it out at G. Wrap the thread over and under the needle point.

Fig 4 Pull the thread through and insert the needle at H and bring it out at I. Wrap the thread over and under the needle point. Pull the thread through and continue working in sequence.

Fig 5 Shows the finished effect of the stitch.

Tulip Head ▶
A trace-off pattern for this design is on page 106

Fern Stitch

This is one of the Straight Stitch forms and is often used to work sprays of fern or other foliage.

The stitch consists of three Straight Stitches of equal length radiating from the same central point.

Fig 1 Bring the thread through at A, insert the needle at B.

Fig 2 Bring the thread through at C, insert the needle at A, through the same hole as before.

Fig 3 Bring the thread through at D and insert the needle again at A.

Fig 4 Bring the thread through at E, insert the needle again at A.

Fig 5 Bring the thread through at F and insert the needle at E.

Fig 6 Bring the thread through at G and insert the needle again at E. With the central stitch following the design line, continue working in sequence.

Fern ▶

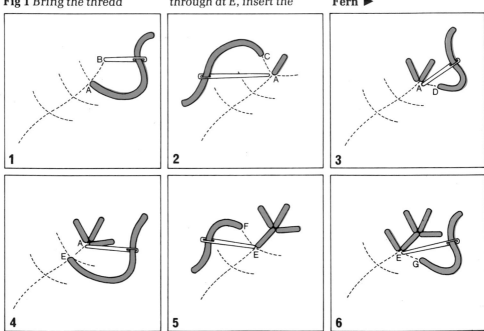

48

Fishbone Stitch

This is a decorative stitch and is usually used to fill leaf shapes, as shown in the Floral Garland design.

Fig 1 Bring the thread through at A and insert the needle at B, making a small, straight stitch along the centre line of the shape.

Fig 2 Bring the needle out at C.

Fig 3 Insert the needle at D next to the base of the first stitch.

Fig 4 Bring the thread through at E and insert at F, overlapping the base of the previous stitch.

Fig 5 Bring the thread through at G and insert the

needle at H, so that the thread lies close to the parallel, sloping stitch and also overlaps the base of the previous stitch.

Fig 6 Continue working sloping stitches, alternating on each side.

Floral Garland ▶

A trace-off pattern for this design is on page 113

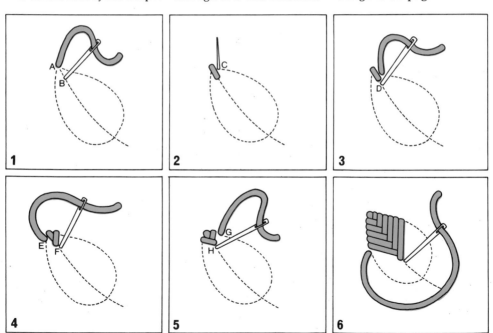

50

Fishbone Stitch, Open

This is a more open version of the stitch on page 50 and is used for leaf shapes when a lighter effect is required in a design. Used for the leaves on the Birds in Flowers design on the opposite page, the stitch contrasts effectively with the solid, Satin Stitch areas.

Fig 1 Bring the thread through at A and insert the needle at B to form a small sloping stitch.

Fig 2 Bring the needle out at C.

Fig 3 Insert the needle at D.

Fig 4 Bring the needle out at E.

Fig 5 Insert the needle at F.

Fig 6 Continue in this way, working sloping stitches alternately on each side, until the shape is filled, spacing stitches evenly.

Birds in Flowers ▶
A trace-off pattern for this design is on page 112

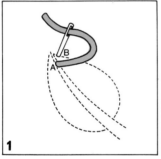

1

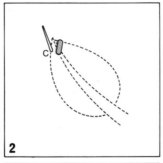

2

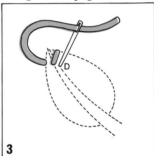

3

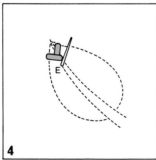

4

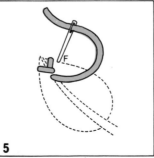

5

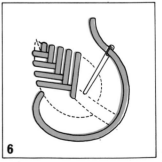

6

Flat Stitch

A variation on the Fishbone Stitches, Flat Stitch has a closer texture and a slightly raised appearance. It has been used to work the flower petals in the design pictured with Chain Stitch for outlining and French Knot stamens.

To guide the placing of stitches, draw two lines down the centre of the shape as shown.

Fig 1 Bring the thread through at A and insert the needle at B on the centre guide line.

Fig 2 Bring the needle out at C on the design line.

Fig 3 Insert the needle at D on the centre guide line.

Fig 4 Bring the needle out at E.

Fig 5 Insert the needle at F.

Fig 6 Continue working alternately from left and right.

Flowers and Butterfly ▶
A trace-off pattern for this design is on page 98

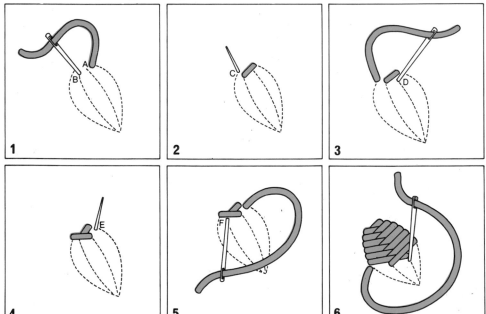

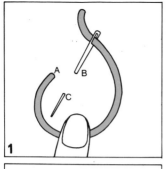

1

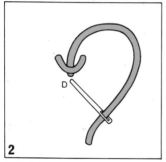

2

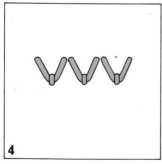

4

Fly Stitch

Fly Stitch is a single, looped stitch which can be used singly, scattered on a design, in rows as a border, or as a filling. The stitch has been used to fill the palm tree shapes in the design pictured on the opposite page.

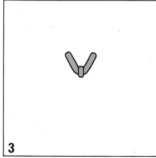

3

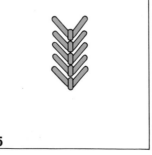

5

Satin Stitch has been used for the solid areas of the design with Fly Stitch for the palm leaves and the flying birds.

Work the design in Stranded Cotton, colours 0311, 0187, 0189, 0266, 0267, 0874, 0907.

Fig 1 *Bring the thread through at A, hold it down with the thumb, insert the needle a little to the right on the same level at B and bring it through at C. (C is midway between A and B.)*

Fig 2 *Keeping the thread under the needle point, pull the thread through. Insert the needle at D to make a small tying stitch in the centre. The length of the tying stitch can be adjusted to suit the requirements of the design.*

Fig 3 *A finished stitch.*

Fig 4 *Fly Stitches can be worked in rows.*

Fig 5 *Fly Stitches worked one above the other. The width of the stitches can be varied to fill a shape.*

Palm Trees ▶
A trace-off pattern for this design is on page 114

1

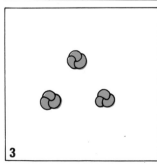

2

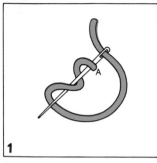

3

French Knot

French Knots can be worked singly and used as spots or dots in a design, or massed together to make a textured area. Used as an outline stitch, French Knots can soften a line and the effect of this can be seen in the Clown and Bear motif on the opposite page. The Bear's outline has been worked in French Knots to depict the softness of fur.

The Clown's hair has been worked with massed French Knots and this textural effect is also used sometimes when animals' fleeces or furs are being interpreted in a design.

Clown and Bear

This design would appeal to children and could be worked as a picture for framing or would make a charming embroidered greetings card.

It is also a suitable motif for children's clothes, perhaps worked on the front of a playsuit or dungarees. The Clown and Bear could be enlarged to form the

main motif in an embroidered bedcover design. Stranded Cotton in the following colours was used to work the design pictured: 0901, 0291, 0304, 0334, 0403, 0110, 0433, 0187 and 0256.

Fig 1 *Bring the thread through at A, the place where the Knot is to be positioned. Encircle the thread twice with the needle.*

Fig 2 *Holding the thread firmly with the thumb, twist the needle back to A and insert it close to where the thread first emerged.*

Fig 3 *Holding the Knot down with the thumb, pull the thread through at the back and secure it with a small stitch for a single French Knot.*

Clown and Bear ▶

A trace-off pattern for this design is on page 115

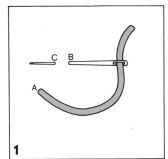

1

Herringbone Stitch

This stitch has numerous uses; it can be worked in single rows as a border, which can then be laced or threaded with contrasting threads or several rows, massed together, make decorative bands for clothing or furnishings. Other stitches, such as Fly Stitch or Chain Stitch can be interspersed between rows.

Herringbone Stitch is also used as a filling stitch and the effect of this can be seen in the design on the opposite page. The cones are worked in rows of Herringbone Stitches to emphasise the pictorial effect of the design.

Fig 1 *Bring the thread through at A on the lower design line. Insert the needle at B on the upper design line and bring it out at C.*

Fig 2 *Insert the needle at D on the lower design line, bringing the needle out at E.*

Fig 3 *Insert the needle at F on the upper design line, bringing it out at G.*

Fig 4 *Insert the needle on the lower design line at H and bring it out at I.*

Fig 5 *Continue working in sequence.*

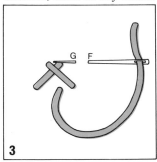

2

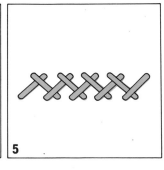

3

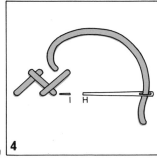

4

5

Icecream Cones ▶
A trace-off pattern for this design is on page 108

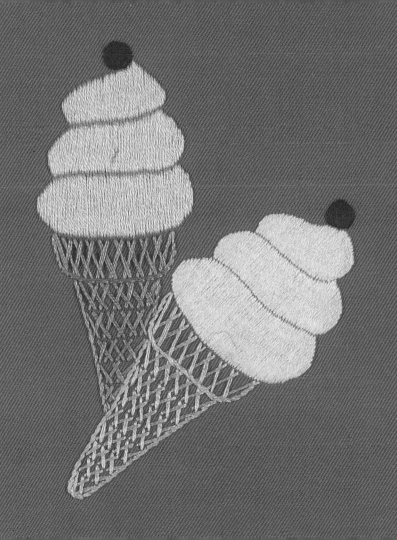

Herringbone Stitch, Closed

Also known as Double Back Stitch, Closed Herringbone Stitch is used for Shadow Work on fine, semi-transparent fabrics. In the diagrams, the formation of the threads on the wrong side of the fabric is shown with broken lines.

Fig 1 Bring the thread through at A, take a small Back Stitch and insert the needle at B.

Fig 2 Bring the thread through at C and insert the needle at D.

Fig 3 Bring the thread through at E and insert the needle at A.

Fig 4 Bring the thread through at F and insert the needle at C.

Fig 5 Bring the thread through at G and insert the needle at E.

Fig 6 The effect of the stitch on the wrong side of fabric.

Tulips ▶
A trace-off pattern for this design is on page 116

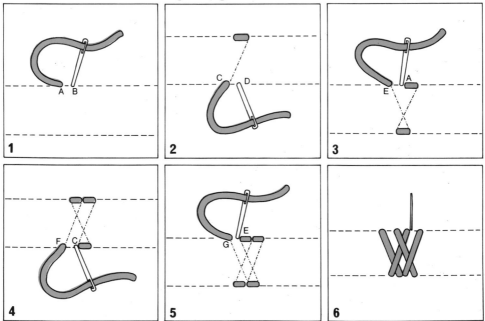

62

Leaf Stitch

As its name suggests, Leaf Stitch is often used to work leaves in designs, as shown in the Butterfly motif on the opposite page but can also be used to fill other shapes. Back Stitch has been used to outline the butterfly and Satin Stitch is worked in the solid areas of the design.

Fig 1 Bring the thread through at A and insert the needle at B to form a sloping stitch.

Fig 2 Bring the needle out at C.

Fig 3 Insert the needle at D.

Fig 4 Bring the needle out at E.

Fig 5 Insert the needle at F.

Fig 6 Continue in this sequence, working stitches alternately on each side until the shape is filled, spacing stitches evenly.

Butterfly ▶
A trace-off pattern for this design is on page 117

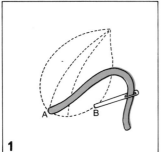

1

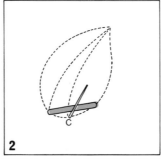

2

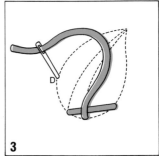

3

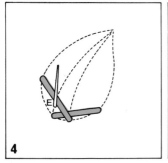

4

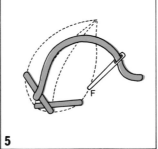

5

6

Long and Short Stitch

This stitch is used for shaded effects in a design. The effect can be seen on the flower petals on the opposite page. The length of stitches can be adjusted to fit a given shape.

Fig 1 Bring the thread through at A and insert the needle at B.

Fig 2 To make a longer stitch, bring the needle through at C.

Fig 3 Insert the needle at D so that the thread lies close to the previous stitch.

Fig 4 Making a short stitch, bring the thread through at E and insert the needle at F, keeping the thread close to the previous stitch.

Fig 5 To work the second row, bring the thread through at G and insert the needle at H.

Fig 6 The third row is worked as the second, with stitches fitting into the preceding row.

Lilies ▶
A trace-off pattern for this design is on page 116

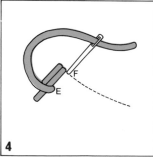

1

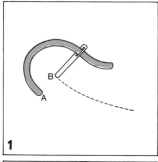

2

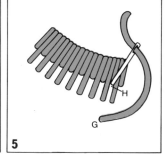

3

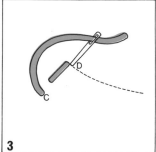

4

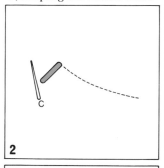

5

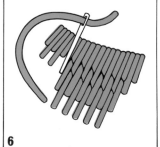

6

Mountmellick Stitch

Mountmellick Stitch takes its name from the White-work embroidery originating in Ireland.

Fig 1 Bring the thread through at A, insert the needle at B and bring out at C. Then pass the needle under the stitch just made, without piercing the fabric.

Fig 2 Pull thread through then re-insert the needle at A and bring it out at C, keeping the thread under the needle point.

Fig 3 Pull the thread through, insert the needle at D, bring it out at E.

Fig 4 Pulling the thread through, pass the needle under the last stitch.

Fig 5 Pull the thread through and re-insert the needle at C, bringing it out again at E, the thread under the needle point.

Fig 6 The finished effect of the stitch.

Lotus Flowers ▶
A trace-off pattern for a flower is on page 118

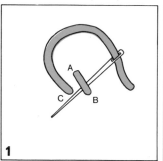

1

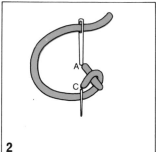

2

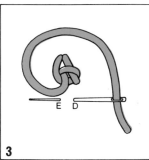

3

4

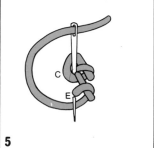

5

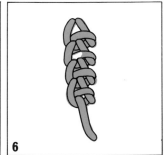

6

Overcast Stitch

Overcast Stitch, also known as Trailing Stitch, is found in forms of Whitework embroidery – Ayrshire work from Scotland, Carrickmacross lace from Ireland and in Broderie Anglaise. It is a couching, or laid thread technique and in the Fish design has been used as an outlining stitch.

Fish
The motif could be worked on a set of guest towels or on a tray cloth or buffet runner. It is also suitable for decorating casual clothing such as summer shirts and tops, and the fish would also make an attractive motif on a towelling robe, worked on a smooth surfaced fabric and afterwards appliquéd in position.

Satin Stitch has been used for the areas of solid colour.

Work the design in Stranded Cotton in the following colours: 0433, 0410, 0295, 0298, 0303, 0304, 0307, 0308, 0148, 0150.

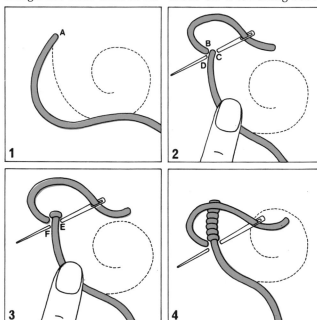

Fig 1 *Bring the laid thread through at A.*

Fig 2 *Hold the laid thread down with the thumb and bring the working thread through at B. Insert the needle at C and, passing the needle under the laid thread to make the stitch, bring it out at D.*

Fig 3 *Pull the thread through and insert the needle at E and bring it out at F to make the second stitch, positioning it close to the previous stitch. Continue making small stitches over the laid thread.*

Fig 4 *The finished effect of Overcasting.*

Fish ▶
A trace-off pattern for this design is on page 111

Raised Rose

Raised Rose is a little known stitch but is ideally suited for working rose flower forms.

Fig 1 Bring the thread through at A and insert the needle at B to form a loop about 3mm (1/8in) high.

Fig 2 Bring the thread through at C and insert the needle at D to form a second loop.

Fig 3 Make two more loops, then work a small Back Stitch at the base of the loops to secure the thread.

Fig 4 Work loose Stem Stitches (see page 90), round the central cluster of loops to form 'petals'.

Fig 5 Continue working Stem Stitch 'petals', reducing the height of the rose towards the outer edge.

Fig 6 The top and side views of a finished Rose.

Flower Spray ▶
A trace-off pattern for this design is on page 118

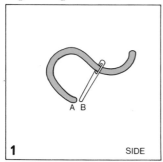

1 SIDE

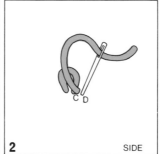

2 SIDE

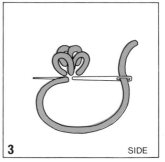

3 SIDE

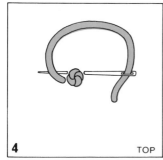

4 TOP

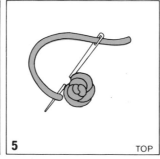

5 TOP

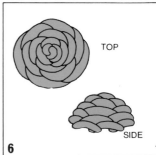

6 TOP / SIDE

72

Raised Chain Band

This stitch produces a thick, raised effect when worked in close rows.

Fig 1 Work a row of closely-spaced horizontal Straight Stitches to the required length for foundation bars.

Fig 2 Bring the thread through at A then, without piercing the fabric, pass the needle upwards under the first bar, and to the left of A.

Fig 3 Pass the needle under the bar, without piercing the fabric, to the right of A, keeping the thread under the needle, and pull through to form a loop.

Fig 4 Insert the needle upwards to the left under the second bar, without piercing the fabric.

Fig 5 Insert the needle downwards under the same bar, keeping the thread under the needle point.

Fig 6 The finished effect.

Twisted Ropes ▶
A trace-off pattern for this design is on page 120

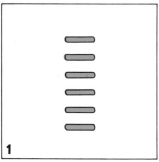

1

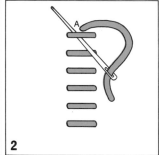

2

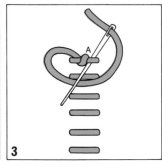

3

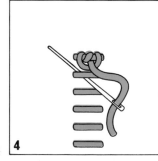

4

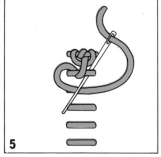

5

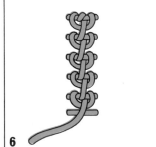

6

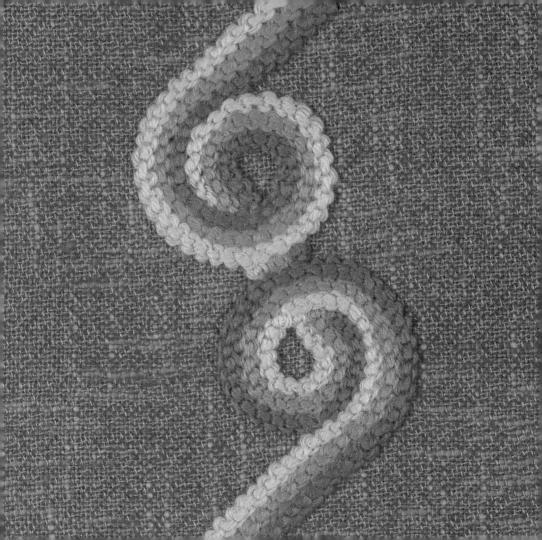

Ribbed Wheel Filling

This stitch is created on an odd number of 'spokes'.

Fig 1 Bring the thread through at A and insert the needle across the circle, but slightly off-centre, at B.

Fig 2 Work three more Straight Stitches, following the sequence C-D, E-F, finishing at G-H.

Fig 3 Bring the thread through at I. Using a tapestry needle, pass the needle under the four Centre Stitches without piercing the fabric. Wrap the thread over and under the needle point.

Fig 4 Pull the thread up to form a centre knot. Pass the needle under spokes F and C without piercing the fabric.

Fig 5 Pull the thread through and pass the needle back over spoke C and under spoke G.

Fig 6 Continue in this way.

Floral Scroll ▶
A trace-off pattern for this design is on page 123

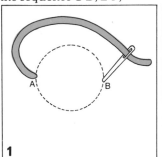

1

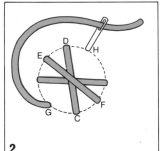

2

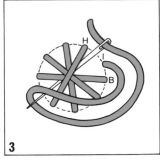

3

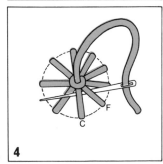

4

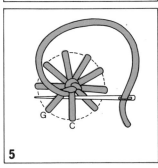

5

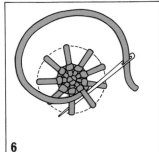

6

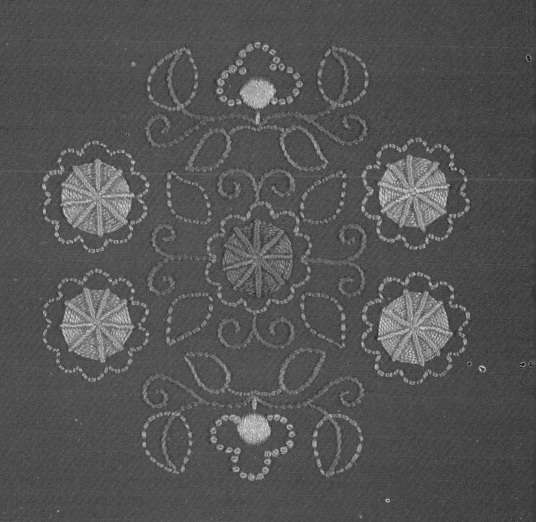

Rope Stitch

This stitch produces an attractive outlining stitch which looks rather like rope. The effect can be seen in the Spring Flowers design on the opposite page. The stitch has been used to outline the leaves and this contrasts effectively with the Satin Stitch stems.

Satin Stitch has also been used to work the flower petals, with massed French Knots for the flower centres.

Spring Flowers

This fresh, pretty design can be used on all kinds of home furnishings and linens. Worked on a pale fabric, the flowers would look good on a set of matched cushions, or could be used on the edges of a round, or square, table-cloth. The design is also suitable for working on guest towels.

Fig 1 *Bring the thread through at A, insert the needle at B and bring it out at C on the design line, twisting the thread over and under the needle point.*

Fig 2 *To set the stitch, pull the thread downwards firmly to form a twisted loop and then pull up to form a second, twisted loop.*

Fig 3 *Insert the needle again at B and bring it out at D, with the thread under the needle point.*

Fig 4 *The effect of the finished stitch with its rope-like formation.*

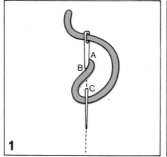

1

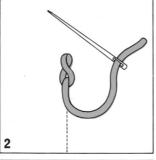

2

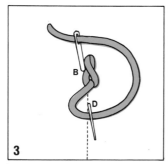

3

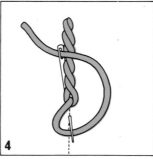

4

Spring Flowers ▶
A trace-off pattern for this design is on page 122

78

Romanian Stitch

This stitch is also referred to as Romanian Couching and, like Bokhara Stitch (pages 6-7), uses the same thread for the laid thread and the couching. Romanian Stitches can be worked to varying lengths to fill a shape such as the leaves in the design opposite.

Fig 1 *Bring the thread through at A, insert the needle at B and bring it out at C.*

Fig 2 *Insert the needle at D and bring it out at E on the guide line.*

Fig 3 *Insert the needle at F and bring it out at G.*

Fig 4 *Insert the needle at H and bring it out at I.*

Fig 5 *Insert the needle at J and bring it out at K.*

Fig 6 *Continue working in sequence.*

Oriental Flower ▶
A trace-off pattern for this design is on page 121

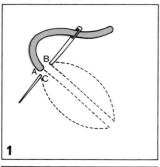

1

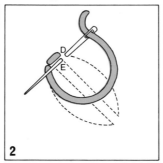

2

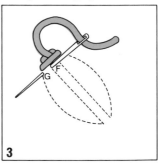

3

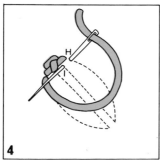

4

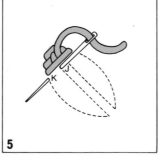

5

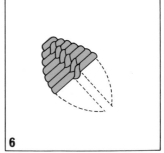

6

Satin Stitch

Satin Stitch is a suitable stitch for filling in the solid areas of a design and, although it is basically a simple stitch to work, consisting entirely of Straight Stitches, it takes practice to get the surface smooth and the edges even.

Hydrangeas

The effect of the Hydrangea design is achieved not only by the use of a toning range of colours but also by the way the Satin Stitches have been worked. By setting the stitches in petals at different angles the light is reflected off in different ways, enhancing the depth of the colours.

Flower designs can also be used effectively on fashion clothes and this circular motif could be positioned on the shoulder of a classic blouse or dress. It is also ideal for decorating garments such as an evening jacket or a bolero, the motif positioned where real flowers might be worn.

The Hydrangeas design pictured is worked in Stranded Cotton in colours 0108, 0109, 0104, 0117, 0118, 0215.

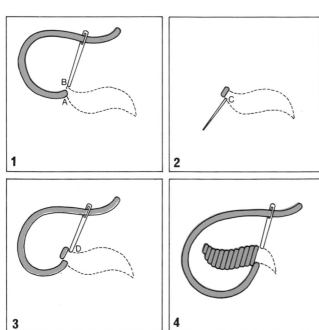

Fig 1 *Bring the thread through at A and insert the needle at B.*

Fig 2 *Bring the needle out at C.*

Fig 3 *Insert the needle at D.*

Fig 4 *Continue in sequence, placing stitches close together so that no background fabric shows through and keeping the edges of the shape even and neat.*

Hydrangeas ▶

A trace-off pattern for this design is on page 119

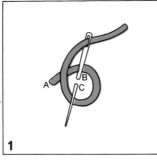

1

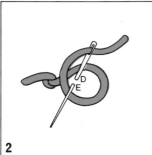

2

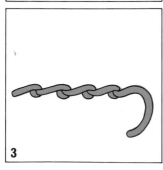

3

Scroll Stitch

This is one of the knotted stitches and makes a very interesting outlining stitch, adding texture to a simple, linear design, such as the Scroll Border on the opposite page. Scroll Stitch could also be used in conjunction with other stitches to make decorative bands (see pages 32–33 and 44–45).

Soft Embroidery Cotton in colour 0129 has been used to work the design pictured.

Scroll Border

The border and corner would work effectively on a square tablecloth or on a traycloth, or could be used on a place mat.

To work such a border on towels, work the embroidery on pre-shrunk fabric first and then stitch the embroidered fabric to the towel ends.

The design can also be worked in other outlining stitches, such as Chain Stitch or Double Knot Stitch, and could be ad- apted for other decorative needlework techniques, such as quilting.

Fig 1 *Bring the needle through at A and insert the needle at B and bring it out at C. Wrap the thread behind the needle and under the point and pull the needle through to form the stitch.*

Fig 2 *Insert the needle at D and bring it out at E, wrapping the thread behind the needle and under the point. Continue in this sequence.*

Fig 3 *The finished effect of the stitch.*

Scroll Border ▶

A trace-off pattern for this design is on page 124

84

Spider's Web Filling

This stitch produces a circular shape which can be used to depict flowers, such as those in the Leaf design opposite, or simply round shapes as a design component.

Leafy Scroll
The motif is designed to be worked on a corner, such as on a tray cloth, buffet runner or a tablecloth, but could also be adapted for a dress neckline or for the corner of a square scarf.

The design pictured is worked in Stranded Cotton colours 0324, 0326, 0340 and 010, with the Spider's Web Fillings worked in Pearl Cotton, colour 011.

French Knots are worked around each of the Spider's Web Fillings to 'lighten' the edge of the circles.

Fig 1 *Bring the thread through at A and insert the needle at B with the thread under the needle point. (A and B are one-fifth of the circumference apart.) Bring the needle through at C in the centre of the circle.*

Fig 2 *Insert the needle at D and bring it out at E (midway between D and A).*

Fig 3 *Insert the needle at the side of C, to make a Straight Stitch, and then bring the thread through at F, and re-insert the needle at the side of C. To secure the thread, bring the thread through at the side of C.*

Fig 4 *To commence weaving, use a tapestry needle, (which has a rounded point), and weave the thread over and under the 'spokes' of the web until the circle is filled.*

Leafy Scroll ▶
A trace-off pattern for this design is on page 123

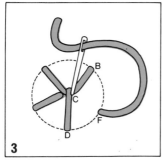

1

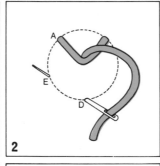

2

3

4

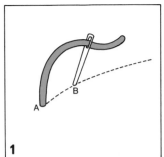

1

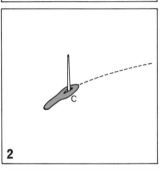

Split Stitch

Split Stitch is worked as a series of Straight Stitches, except that when the needle comes through the fabric it pierces the thread of the previous stitch. Split Stitch can be used as a delicate outlining stitch but it can also be used in rows as a filling stitch.

Doves and Flowers

The design pictured is worked in French Knots and Satin Stitch, as well as Split Stitch which is used to outline the Doves. Stranded Cotton in the following colours is used: 01, 0301, 0264, 0265, 0386, 0388, 0397, 0392.

Fig 1 Bring the thread through at A and insert the needle at B.

Fig 2 Bring the needle through at C, piercing the thread of the previous stitch.

Fig 3 Insert the needle at D to form the next stitch.

Fig 4 Bring the needle through at E, piercing the previous stitch and insert it at F to form the next stitch.

Fig 5 The effect of Split Stitch. The length of the stitch can vary according to the effect desired.

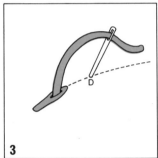

3

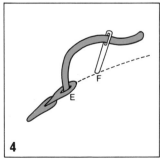

4 (image 4)

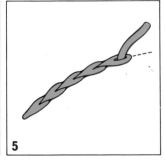

5

Doves and Flowers ▶
A trace-off pattern for this design is on page 124

Stem Stitch

Stem Stitch is one of the most popular outlining stitches but it is also the stitch most often chosen for working stems of flowers. If a thicker Stem Stitch is required for a design, make the angle at which the stitch is taken greater (see Fig 1, B-C).

Bowl of Flowers

The design is an ideal subject for a framed picture or an embroidered greetings card, but it could also be enlarged to be worked on a cushion.

Satin Stitch is used for the solid areas of the design, with Stem Stitch used for some of the outlines. Detached Chain Stitch daisies add texture to the overall design.

The design pictured is worked in Stranded Cotton in these colours: 01, 0842, 0843, 0301, 0302, 0304, 0158, 0928.

Fig 1 *Bring the thread through on the design line at A and hold it down with the thumb. Insert the needle at B and bring it out at C, midway between A and B.*

Fig 2 *Pull the thread through to set the first stitch. Hold the working thread down with the thumb and insert the needle at D, bringing it out at B.*

Fig 3 *Insert the needle at E and bring it out at D. Continue in this way, making each stitch exactly the same length.*

Fig 4 *The effect of the stitch.*

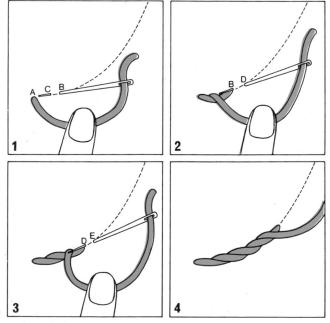

Bowl of Flowers

A trace-off pattern for this design is on page 126

Straight Stitch

This stitch is the simplest of all the free-style stitches and has a variety of applications and uses. In the diagrams, (Figs 1 and 2), Straight Stitches are shown worked into a daisy formation, while in the design opposite – Daffodils – the stitches are used as a filling for the petals.

Straight Stitches can be worked in varying lengths, overlapping, vertical, slanting or horizontal, and are one of the most versatile of stitches in embroidery.

Daffodils
This simple design would make a charming border, repeated along the edge of a buffet runner or at the ends of a tray cloth or trolley cloth. Used at the size depicted, it could be worked on a small cushion or, enlarged photographically, for a larger furnishing accessory.

These daffodils could also be interpreted in other embroidery techniques, such as appliqué or quilting.

Satin Stitch has been used for the solid areas of the design, the leaves and the daffodil trumpets, with Stem Stitch for some of the outlined areas. French Knots make the stamens. Stranded Cotton in these colours is used: 0293, 0297, 0298, 0304, 0280 and 0281.

Fig 1 Bring the thread through at A and insert the needle at B. Bring the needle through at C and re-insert it at D. Bring the needle through at E and insert it again at F. In this formation, Straight Stitches are of irregular length.

Fig 2 Work Straight Stitches from A to B, at the centre of the design, then from C to B, D to B, E to B and so on, keeping all the stitches to the same length. Finish stitches on the wrong side of work with a small Back Stitch.

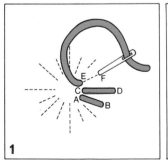

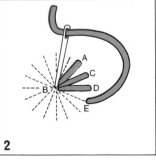

1

2

92

Daffodils ▶
A trace-off pattern for this design is on page 127

Vandyke Stitch

This is an attractive filling stitch, often used for leaf shapes, although it can also be worked as a decorative border.

The Flower motif on the opposite page has Vandyke Stitches worked on the leaf shapes, together with Stem Stitch, Satin Stitch, Back Stitch and French Knots for other parts of the design.

Fig 1 Bring the thread through at A and take a small stitch from B to C.

Fig 2 Pull the thread taut and insert the needle at D (on the same level as A) and bring through at E.

Fig 3 Without piercing the fabric, pass the needle under the crossed threads.

Fig 4 Pull the thread taut and insert the needle at F (on the same level as E), and bring it out at G.

Fig 5 Continue, following Figs 3 and 4.

Fig 6 The finished effect.

Jacobean Flower ▶
A trace-off pattern for this design is on page 125

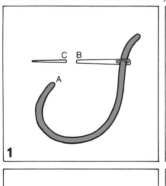

1

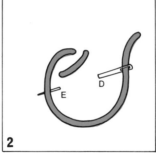

2

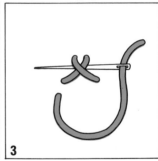

3

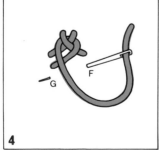

4

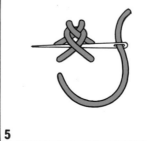

5

6

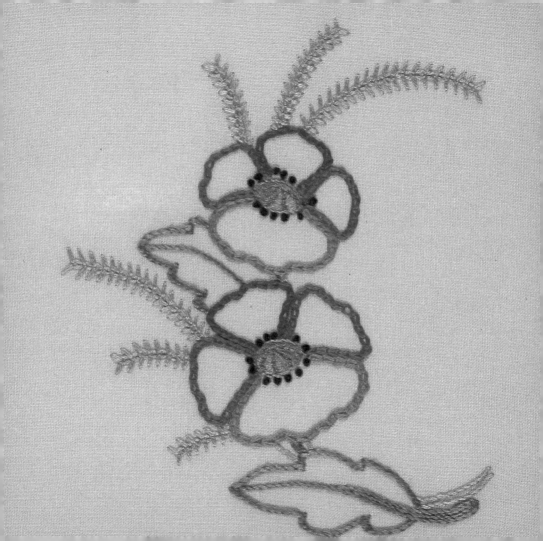

Wheatear Stitch

This is one of the looped stitches and, properly worked with even tension, looks rather like the formation of an ear of wheat.

In the Poppies and Wheat design on the opposite page, the realistic effect of the stitch can be seen.

Fig 1 *Bring the thread through at A and insert the needle at B. Bring the needle out at C.*

Fig 2 *Insert the needle at D and bring it out at E.*

Fig 3 *Without piercing the fabric, pass the needle under the two Straight Stitches.*

Fig 4 *Insert the needle at F and bring it out at G.*

Fig 5 *Insert the needle at F and bring it out at H. Continue working in sequence.*

Fig 6 *The finished stitch.*

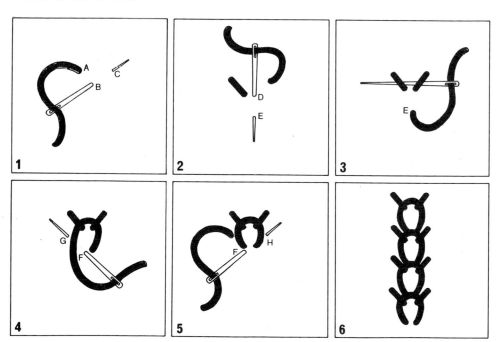

Flower Edging
page 3

98

**Flowers and
Butterfly**
page 55

Happy Bear
page 7 (half motif)

Emily with Flowers 99
page 35

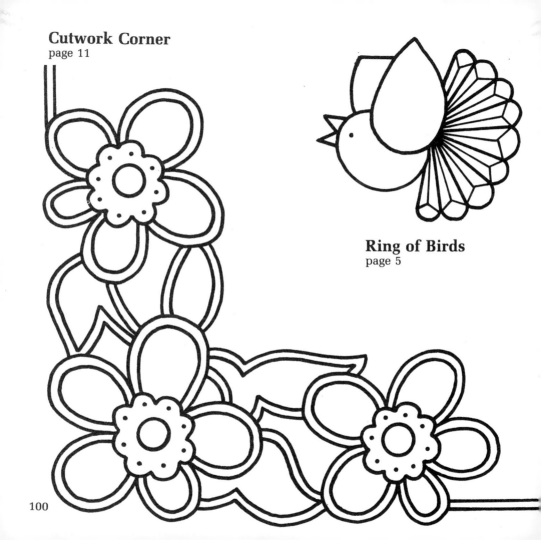

Cutwork Corner
page 11

Ring of Birds
page 5

Cutwork Butterfly
page 13

Corner Scroll
page 15

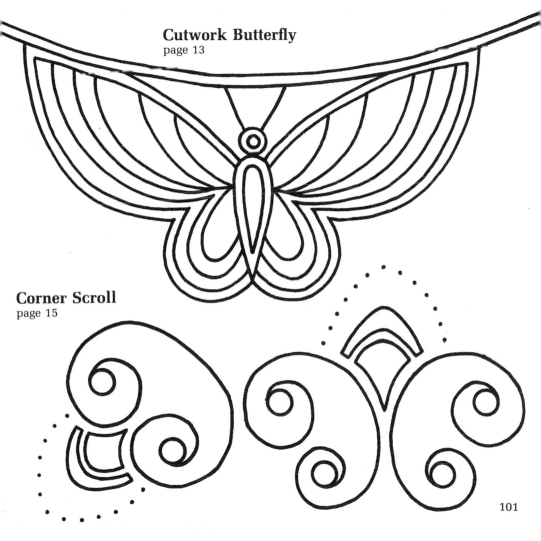

Girl with Balloons
page 9

Basket of Flowers
page 39

102

Aeroplanes
page 21

103

Little House
page 19

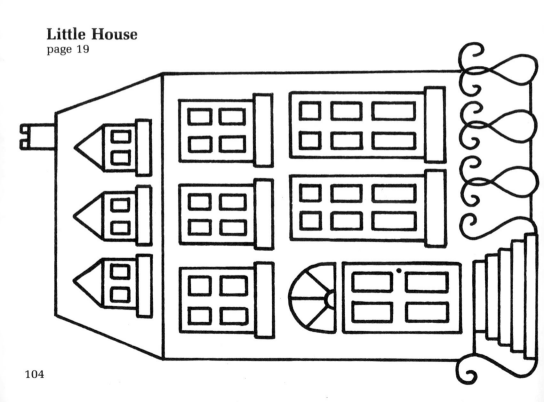

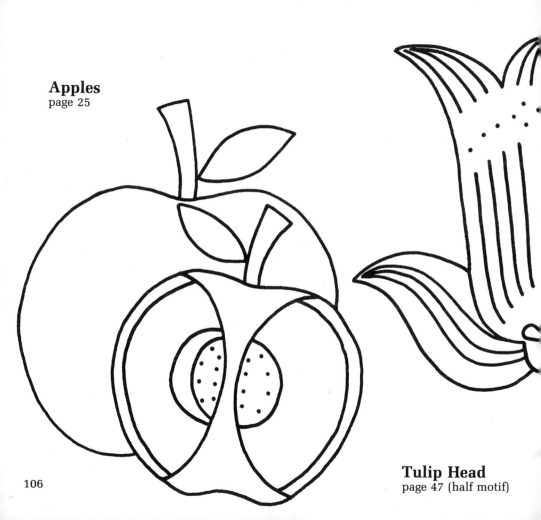

Apples
page 25

Tulip Head
page 47 (half motif)

106

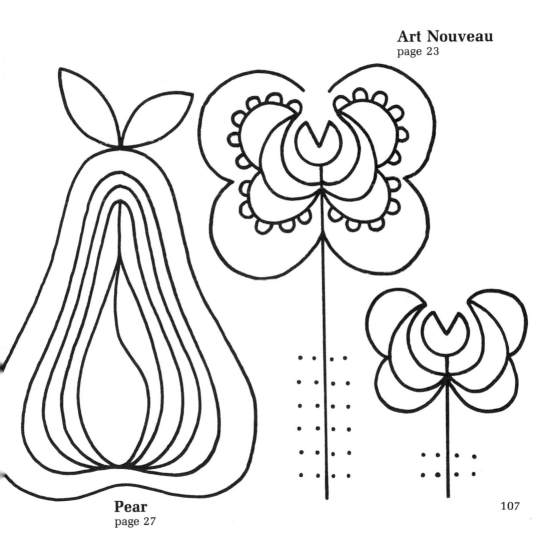

Pear
page 27

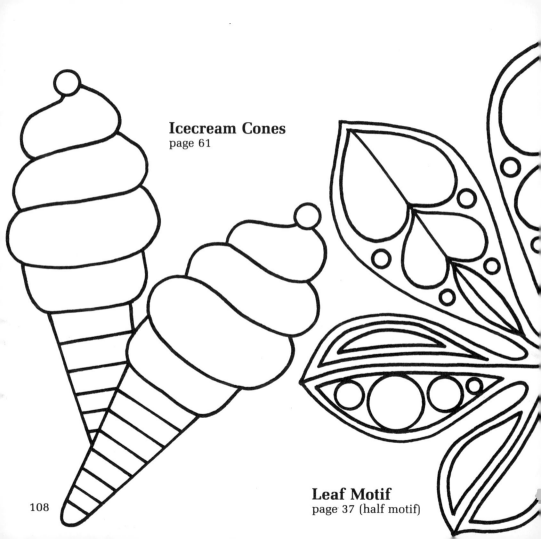

Icecream Cones
page 61

Leaf Motif
page 37 (half motif)

108

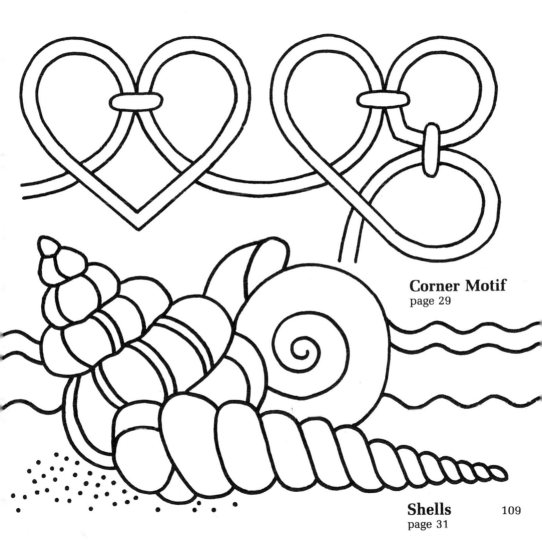

Corner Motif
page 29

Shells 109
page 31

Leaf Border
page 41

Scroll Motif
page 43

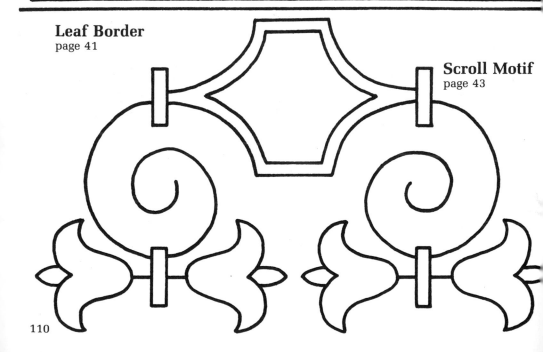

Fish
page 71

111

Floral Garland
page 51

113

Palm Trees
page 57

Clown and Bear
page 59

115

Tulips
page 63

Lilies
page 67

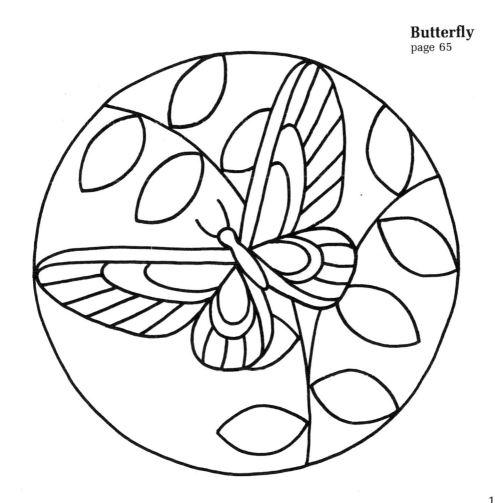

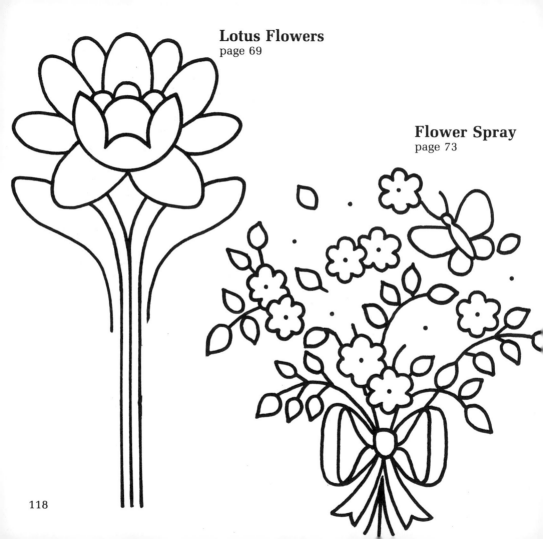

Lotus Flowers
page 69

Flower Spray
page 73

118

Hydrangeas
page 83

Twisted Ropes
page 75

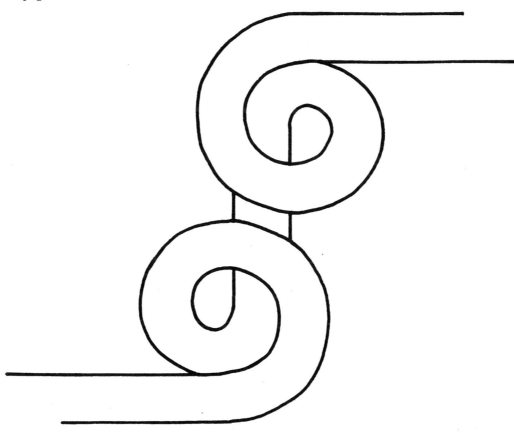

Spring Flowers
page 79

Leafy Scroll
page 87

Floral Scroll
page 77 (half motif)

123

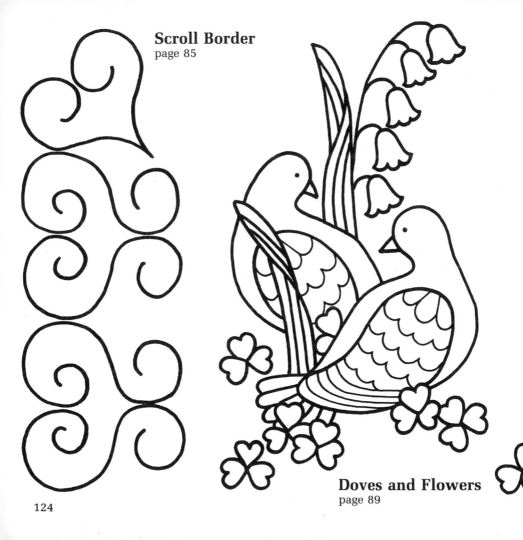

Scroll Border
page 85

Doves and Flowers
page 89

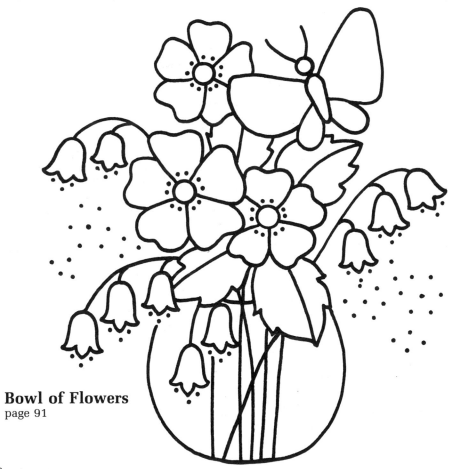

Bowl of Flowers
page 91

Daffodils
page 93

British Library Cataloguing in Publication Data

The New anchor book of embroidery stitches.
  No. 1: Free-style stitches and motifs
  1. Embroidery
  1. Harlow, Eve
  746.44'042   TT770

  ISBN 0-7153-8861-4

First published 1987
Reprinted 1987, 1989, 1990, 1991, 1992

© Text: David & Charles plc 1987
© Illustrations by Jill Shipley: J.&P. Coats (UK) Ltd

Phototypeset by Typesetters (Birmingham) Ltd,
Smethwick, West Midlands
and printed in Italy
by New Interlitho, Milan
for David & Charles plc
Brunel House   Newton Abbot   Devon